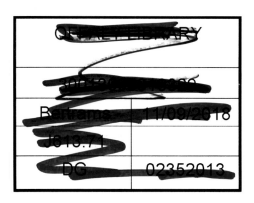

Bear Grylls

SURVIVAL SKILLS HANDBOOK

EXERCISE

Bear Grylls

This survival skills handbook has been specially put together to help young adventurers like you to stay safe in the wild. Staying fit and healthy is not only a key part of any expedition, it is a vital part of everyday life. You should try to do at least some exercise every day. This book will give you lots of helpful hints and tips on how to exercise to keep your body in tip-top shape... all while having a lot of fun at the same time!

Bear

CONTENTS

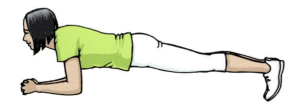

WHY EXERCISE?

Exercise is vital to keep your body strong and healthy. Not only does having a good level of fitness make expeditions much easier and more enjoyable, it could mean the difference between life and death in a survival situation.

Benefits of exercise

In days gone by, people were a lot more active in their day-to-day lives. Now, we spend much more time sitting down, and need to exercise more to make up for this. As well as keeping your body healthy, regular exercise can be very good for you in some surprising ways.

Boosts brain power

When you exercise, it boosts the supply of oxygen-rich blood to your brain. This improves co-ordination, helps with memory, and increases your ability to concentrate.

Energizes, yet relaxes

Exercise speeds up your metabolism – the rate at which your body burns fuel for energy. This energizes you and makes you more alert. Surprisingly, exercise also relaxes you and helps you sleep.

Helps you feel good

Exercise causes the brain to release chemicals called "endorphins", which make you feel happy. This is your brain's way of telling you that what you are doing is great, and encouraging you to keep doing it. Exercise can really lift your mood when you are feeling low – and the feeling can stick around all day!

Prevents illness

Exercise boosts your immune system, the parts of your body which fight germs, keeping illness at bay. Doctors say taking regular exercise reduces your risk of developing all sorts of diseases, including heart disease, diabetes, and even some cancers, as you get older.

Improves your social life

Getting involved in team sports or exercise classes is a great way to meet people and make new friends. It can also boost your self-confidence, as well as improving your ability to work as part of a team.

BONES AND MUSCLES

All movement in your body is caused by muscles, which are attached to the bones of the skeleton by fibres called tendons. Understanding how the body works is important to fitness training, as this will help you know what muscle groups to work out and how.

Muscle network

Your entire body is covered with a complex network of muscles, attached to the bones at joints by rubbery strings called tendons. This diagram shows some of the main muscle groups used during exercise.

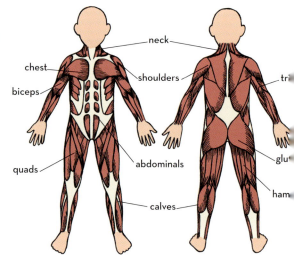

neck

chest

shoulders

biceps

tri

quads

abdominals

glu

ham

calves

Muscle pairs

Muscles are arranged in pairs on opposite sides of bones. They work by alternately contracting and relaxing to pull the bone in different ways. In the upper arm, the bicep muscle contracts and the tricep relaxes as you bend your elbow. The bicep relaxes and the tricep contracts to straighten the elbow.

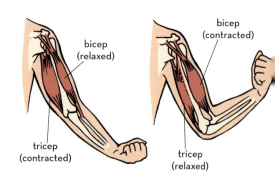

bicep
(relaxed)

bicep
(contracted)

tricep
(contracted)

tricep
(relaxed)

How muscles work

Muscles are bundles of long, thin fibres. They work by contracting (getting shorter) and then relaxing, which allows another muscle to contract.

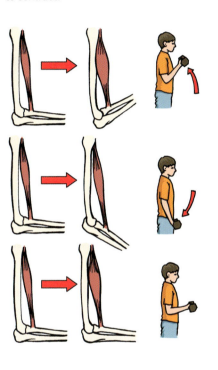

BEAR SAYS

Gentle, jolting exercise such as skipping, jumping, and hopping makes bones grow denser and stronger. This means you're less likely to break a bone if you fall.

Muscles and exercise

Lack of exercise makes muscles weak. Regular exercise makes them bigger and stronger. It also strengthens bones and joints, and so makes injury less likely.

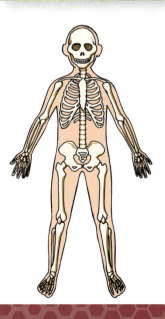

Skeleton

The skeleton is the body's framework. A human skeleton contains over 200 bones, over half of which are in your hands, wrists, feet, and ankles. It is important to look after your skeleton – a broken bone can be very painful and may take a long time to mend.

7

HEART AND CIRCULATION

Your heart, blood, and blood vessels form your circulation system. Your heart pumps blood, which travels, or "circulates", around your whole body, carrying oxygen and nutrients to all parts of your body.

Blood
This is the body's main transport network. It delivers oxygen and energy-rich sugars to every part of the body, including the muscles, and removes waste.

Circulation system
The circulation system is a network of blood vessels stretching throughout the body. Arteries carry oxygen-rich blood from the heart to the body. Arteries divide to form fine blood vessels called capillaries. These then join up to form veins, carrying blood low in oxygen and nutrients back to the heart and lungs.

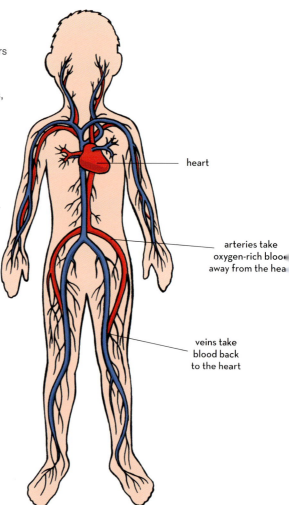

heart

arteries take oxygen-rich blood away from the heart

veins take blood back to the heart

Heart

The heart is a muscular pump that never stops beating. Like other muscles, heart muscles work by contracting. Each contraction sends a little surge of blood along your arteries – this is called a pulse.

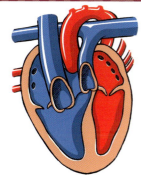

Heart and exercise

When you exercise, your heart pumps faster to deliver blood to your muscles. If you are unfit, strenuous exercise will make your heart pound. Exercise strengthens the heart so it pumps more efficiently. This lowers your heart rate and pulse.

Finding your pulse

Find the pulse at your wrist by pressing two fingers just below the mound of your thumb. Don't use your thumb, as it has its own strong pulse. If you can't find a pulse in your wrist, try checking your neck, just beside the throat.

Measuring your heart rate

Using a watch or stopwatch, count the number of times your heart beats in a minute. This is called your resting pulse. Measure your pulse again after walking for three minutes, and then after running for three minutes, to see how much it increases. How long does it take to return to your resting pulse?

BEAR SAYS

Time yourself after exercise to find out how long it takes for your heart rate to return to your resting pulse. This is called your recovery rate, and shows how fit you are.

LUNGS AND BREATHING

When you draw air into your lungs, oxygen passes into your bloodstream. Your muscles use oxygen as they pull on bones. Oxygen is also needed to unlock the fuel you get from your food.

Breathing in and out

As you breathe in, air entering your nose and mouth passes down your windpipe into your lungs. Here, oxygen is sucked into tiny air sacs called alveoli, where it is passed into your blood. The waste gas carbon dioxide passes from the blood into your lungs so you can breathe it out. Carbon dioxide is produced as the body uses energy.

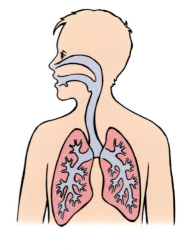

BEAR SAYS

A fit person should be able to carry on a brief conversation during exercise. But if you can sing a song loudly while exercising, you are taking it too easy!

Exchange of gases

Each tiny air sac is surrounded by a network of fine blood vessels. Oxygen seeps through the thin cell wall into the blood, and carbon dioxide seeps out.

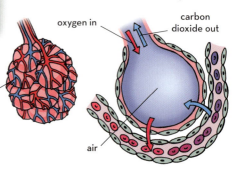

oxygen in

carbon dioxide out

alveoli covered in tiny veins and arteries

air

Breathing and exercise

When you exercise, your lungs work harder to supply muscles with oxygen. If you are unfit, exercise will make you out of breath. As your fitness improves, your breathing will become more efficient.

Asthma

People with asthma have some difficulty breathing. If you are asthmatic, always take your inhaler with you when you exercise. Warm up slowly (see pages 20–21). Talk to your doctor about your exercise programme.

Aerobic exercise

Aerobic means "with oxygen". Aerobic exercises, such as jogging, cycling, and swimming, make the heart and lungs work harder, to improve fitness. The more aerobic exercise you do, the easier you will find it, as your heart and lungs grow stronger.

Anaerobic exercise

Anaerobic means "without oxygen". When you sprint to catch a bus, your body uses oxygen faster than your lungs can supply it, so it releases stored oxygen. Anaerobic exercise such as sprinting makes muscles stronger and more flexible.

EATING FOR FITNESS

Food provides the fuel that your body burns to keep warm and be active. You also need fuel to grow, fight illness, and repair cuts and bruises. Eating a balanced diet is an important part of staying fit and healthy.

Balanced diet

Different foods help the body in different ways. You need to eat the right amount of each type, as shown on this page. Carbohydrates, vegetables, and fruit are the mainstays of a healthy diet. Smaller amounts of protein and a little fat are also necessary for a balanced diet.

Carbohydrates

Starchy foods such as bread, potatoes, pasta, and rice are our main source of energy. These foods release energy slowly to keep you going for longer. Fruit and sweets contain energy in the form of sugar, which is released quickly.

Protein

Protein in meat, fish, eggs, beans, nuts, and dairy builds muscles, repairs injuries, and helps you grow.

BEAR SAYS

Don't exercise too soon after eating, or you could get cramp. Take a bottle of water with you so you can replace fluids during or after exercise.

Fruit and veg

Fruit and vegetables provide vitamins and minerals that are needed for a healthy body, including for strong bones. They also contain fibre, which is good for digestion. You should eat at least five to seven portions (usually a good-sized handful) of fruit and veg every day as part of a balanced diet.

ats

e body needs some fat for health, including keep nerves in good condition, but eating o much fat or sugar is bad for you. Fat can og your arteries, reducing circulation and rcing your heart to work harder. Burgers, chips, oughnuts, cakes, and biscuits are OK for an casional treat, but don't eat them every day if u want to be strong and healthy!

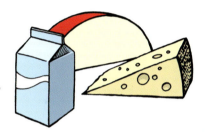

Water

Water is vital for survival. You need to drink at least two litres of water every day to replace fluids lost when you sweat and pee. When you exercise you need to drink even more.

Energy snacks

Eat fruit, nuts, raisins, or sugar-free cereal if you need an energy boost before or after playing sport.

HEALTHY LIFESTYLE

Exercise and a balanced diet are just part of a healthy lifestyle. You also need to cope with any stress or worries, spend time outdoors, get enough sleep, and keep your body fresh and clean.

Dealing with stress

Most people have some stress and worries. Many of us also feel angry and frustrated at times. Talking about your problems can help. Talk to someone your own age or to a trusted adult. Exercise can help to reduce worries and channel anger and frustration.

Get active!

In days gone by, people were often more active than they are now. Most people walked to work or school, and chores such as cleaning the house took a lot of effort. In the modern age of cars, computers, and vacuum cleaners, taking regular exercise is more important than ever for a healthy lifestyle.

Take a break

Nowadays we all spend a lot of time looking at screens on phones, tablets, TVs, or computers. Take a break after a spell in front of a screen. A short walk, run, or cycle will restore energy levels and help you concentrate.

Fresh air and sunshine

The old saying is true – fresh air really is good for you. Time outdoors filling your lungs with fresh air is part of a healthy lifestyle. Sunshine makes the body produce vitamin D, needed for healthy teeth, bones, and muscles. However, too much sun can be harmful, so use sun cream or cover up if you spend a long time in the sun.

Sleep

Sleep is vital for health. It helps the body to repair injury and fight illness, as well as keeping you sharp and alert when you're awake. Avoid excessive tea, coffee, and chocolate, which all contain a chemical called caffeine which keeps you awake, and put away all screens at least half an hour before bedtime for a good night's sleep.

Hygiene

Good hygiene is part of looking after yourself. Have a shower or take a bath every day to freshen up, particularly after you exercise.

THE CHOICE IS YOURS

Exercise isn't just about sport. There are all sorts of ways to stay in shape and be active. Any form of physical activity counts as exercise, so the choice is huge!

Choosing an exercise

Finding the right exercise is important. Many games, dance, martial arts, and even household chores all count as exercise. Do you enjoy being part of a team, or do you prefer to exercise alone or with one or two friends? Choose an activity that suits you. If you try an activity and find it's not for you, don't worry – there are loads of options, so move on and try something else.

Sports

There is a huge range of different sports, including badminton, basketball, trampolining, and archery as well as football, rounders, cricket, hockey, and tennis. Some sports require a whole team of people, while others can be played with two people or even by yourself. Have you considered athletics, golf, orienteering, rowing, fencing, or water polo?

BEAR SAYS

Consider cost and convenience before you opt for an activity. Is it expensive to take part? Do you need special kit? Is the place and time convenient?

Outdoor activities

Outdoor pursuits can be a lot of fun, and include hiking, climbing, canoeing, sledging, biking, roller blading, parkour, surfing, and skateboarding. You could even plan a whole expedition around one or more of these activities.

Dance and gym classes

Most gyms offer group exercise classes, including weight-training, yoga, and aerobics. Dance can also be a fun way of keeping fit – why not try break-dancing, salsa, Bollywood, hip hop, or cheerleading?

Martial arts

Martial arts not only help you keep fit, but they also train you in physical and mental control, as well as showing you how to defend yourself. Some popular martial arts are judo, karate, tai chi, kickboxing, and taekwondo.

Fun and games

Many games, such as skipping, tag, leapfrog, or races, count as exercise. This is a really fun way to stay fit with your friends. Look at pages 42–45 for suggestions of different games to play.

Chores

Chores like gardening, washing the car, vacuuming, tidying your room, and carrying heavy shopping help keep you active and your body trim. Not only that, but you're doing a good deed!

Everyday life

Opt for a bit more exercise in your daily life. For example, why not climb the stairs instead of taking the lift? Can you bike or walk to school, or get off the bus a stop early and walk?

GETTING GOING

So you've decided to do more exercise, or begin training for a new sport. Great! But how exactly do you start? There are lots of things you'll need to know before you start training.

Start small

Don't be overambitious, particularly if it's been a while since you've exercised. Start with some gentle, easy goals, and slowly build up to greater things.

BEAR SAYS

Mastering a new skill takes time. Don't be put off if you're not brilliant straight away. Be patient and keep trying – remember, practice makes perfect.

The right gear

Make sure you have the necessary safety kit before you start. For example, if you want to try skateboarding or cycling, you will need to get a good helmet and possibly elbow and knee pads. The correct footwear is also important for many activities. Having the right gear will help you to avoid injuries and sprains.

How much exercise?

To increase your level of fitness, aim to do at least half an hour's exercise four times a week. The key is little and often, and exercise regularly. You can break up the time into smaller units. For example, you could do 20 minutes sport, 10 minutes circuit training (see pages 40–41), and 10 minutes biking to school.

Challenge yourself

Set yourself a goal and gradually make it harder as your fitness increases. Time yourself using a watch or stopwatch. See if you can beat your previous time, increase your time or distance, or do more of a given exercise inside a minute.

Keep a record

It's a good idea to keep a record of your aims and exercise sessions to chart your progress. Note down dates, times, the type of exercise, and how it went. Some exercise apps help you keep a record. This is a great way of seeing how much fitter you're getting!

Before and after

Always warm up before you start exercising and cool down afterwards – see pages 20–21. This might feel easy, but forgetting to warm up or cool down can cause you to damage your muscles.

WARMING UP

Warm-up exercises send blood to your muscles. This makes them more flexible, so you are less likely to get injured. Do the same exercises more gently as a cool-down routine.

Side stretch

Stand with your feet shoulder-width apart. Bend to one side from your waist. Slide your arm down your leg and feel the stretch in your side. Repeat twice more, then stretch to the other side.

Rotate from waist

Stand with your feet shoulder-width apart and raise your arms to your chest. Gently rotate the body from the waist to the left and look behind you. Try to keep your hips facing forwards. Now rotate the body to the right, and return to the middle. Repeat twice more.

BEAR SAYS

You can also warm up by slowly doing the movements that will be involved in your activity. For example, if playing a racket sport you would slowly swing the racket.

Arm circles

Stand with your feet a little way apart. Slowly circle your right arm backwards, past your ear, forwards, and down. Do this three times, then circle the left arm backwards three times. Repeat, but now circle the right arm forwards, then the left arm.

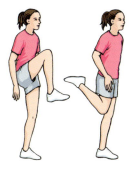

Knee raise

Standing straight, slowly raise one knee to your chest, then slowly swing it down and bring your foot up to your bottom. Make slow, steady movements and try to keep upright. Return to standing position and repeat twice more, then repeat with the other leg.

Foot circles

From a standing or sitting position, raise one foot and slowly move it in a circle. Repeat twice more, then circle the foot in the opposite direction. Repeat with the other foot, in both directions.

Jog on the spot

Gently jog on the spot for a minute while moving your arms in small circles first one way, then the other. This will get your heart beating faster.

AVOIDING INJURY

It is always tempting to push your body as hard as you can when training to get fit, but avoiding injury is vital. Take care of your body and pay attention to any pain, particularly in your joints. If anything starts to hurt – stop! Learn to listen to your body and to adapt your training as necessary. Remember the survival phrase: Improvise, Adapt, Overcome.

Don't overexercise

Some people get so keen on exercise they overdo it, and carry on even if it hurts. This puts excessive strain on the body and can lead to lasting injury. Don't be too tough on yourself, and don't let anyone else put too much pressure on you to perform well. Exercise isn't meant to stress you out!

Illness

Don't exercise if you feel ill, or think you are coming down with a cold or flu. In these situations, exercise will lower your resistance, so give training a miss.

Faint or dizzy

If you feel dizzy or faint during exercise stop, sit down, and rest. Take small sips of water. Don't continue exercising unless you are fully recovered.

BEAR SAYS

A hot shower after exercise can help to ease minor muscle strains. Allow hot water to play on the affected area.

Cramp

Cramp is when a muscle over-contracts or goes into spasm. It can be really painful. Massage the affected area and stretch gently. For a calf cramp, stand on the affected leg.

Using equipment

Lots of sports involve specialist equipment. Check you know how to use any equipment involved properly before you start. For example, you will need to have a proper training session with a professional before using weights in a gym.

Clothing

Don't strip off before you start exercising – warm up first, then take off a layer of clothing. Increased blood circulation during exercise will make you warmer. Put a layer back on as soon as you finish and start to cool down.

Catching your breath

To catch your breath after sprinting, put your hands on your knees and lower your head. In this position, muscles in your neck, shoulders, and chest help return your breathing to normal.

ELEMENTS OF FITNESS

Fitness is made up of three main elements: flexibility, strength, and stamina. Different types of exercise focus on different elements, though you should try to do a little of all three. But what exactly do these mean?

Flexibility

Suppleness, or flexibility, is the ability to move your joints through their full range of movement without straining. In short, it means you're bendy! Improving suppleness helps to keep your body in good shape and  makes you much less likely to strain a muscle. The different stretches on pages 26–31 will help improve flexibility. Doing flexibility-based exercises such gym, yoga, ballet, or martial arts also makes you more supple.

BEAR SAYS

Don't push yourself too hard when you're stretching. If it starts to hurt, stop! Over-stretching a muscle can be very painful and cause injury.

Strength

There are two kinds of strength. The first is the ability to perform feats of strength, such as lifting a heavy weight. The other is being able to repeat a strenuous exercise, such as sit-ups, many times. The exercises on pages 32–37 are designed to increase muscle strength. Gym, athletics, climbing, and weight-training increase muscle strength, as does anaerobic exercise, which makes the body release stored oxygen.

Stamina

Stamina, or endurance, is the ability to keep going with strenuous exercise. Aerobic exercise such as jogging, cycling, or swimming improves stamina by making your heart and lungs work harder. These forms of exercise also burn calories to keep you at a healthy weight. The exercises on pages 38–41 are designed to increase endurance.

BEAR SAYS

Many types of exercise improve more than one of these elements. For example, cycling builds strength and stamina. Badminton, squash, and basketball build all three.

UPPER BODY STRETCHES

Stretching exercises make your muscles more elastic, so you can perform a much wider range of movement. The exercises on this page help to improve flexibility in the neck, arms, and shoulders.

Side neck stretch
Stand straight with your head up. Slowly and gently bend your head to one side, so your ear moves towards your shoulder, until you can feel a gentle stretch in one side of your neck. Hold this for a few seconds. Now gently bend the head to the opposite side. Be careful not to overstretch.

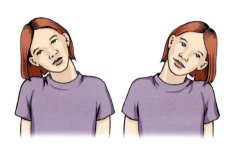

Up and down neck stretch
Stand straight with your head up. Slowly and gently raise your chin as high as it will go, then slowly lower your chin to your chest. This should stretch the back of your neck.

BEAR SAYS

Do these stretches regularly and you will gradually become more supple. Keep notes to record how your flexibility improves.

Chest stretch

Stand with your feet a little way apart. Clasp your hands behind your back and then gently raise them upwards. Keep the arms as straight as possible, with your chest out and shoulders down.

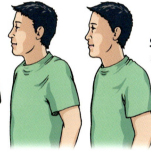

Shoulder stretch

Stand with your feet a little way apart. Raise your shoulders towards your ears, then roll your shoulders backwards and down. Repeat twice more, then roll the shoulders in the opposite direction.

High and low

Stand with your feet a little way apart. Raise both arms above your head and stretch up as high as you can. Then carefully bend from the waist, keeping your chin up. Stretch down towards your toes. Do not overstretch.

Touch your toes

Sit on the floor with your legs stretched out in front of you. Slowly and gently bend forwards and reach for your right foot with your right arm. Keep your back straight and stomach pulled in. Come back up, then stretch your left hand towards your left foot.

LOWER BODY STRETCHES

The exercises on this page focus on the lower body, especially the hips and legs, to make this part of your body more flexible.

Calf stretch

Take one big step forward, so one foot is about a metre in front of the other. With both feet facing forwards, bend the front knee, keeping the heel of the back foot on the ground. Keep the body upright. You should be able to feel the stretch in the back leg, along the calf muscle – the muscle along the back of your leg. Hold this position for a few seconds, then take another pace forward, and stretch the other leg.

Side leg raise

Lie on your left side with your left hand supporting the head and your right hand in front of your chest to help with balance. Raise a straight right leg as high as it will go. Lower and raise twice more. Now lie on your right side and raise your left leg.

BEAR SAYS

Make sure you gently stretch the muscles you will be using before and after any exercise. Hold all stretches for 15-30 seconds.

Quad stretch

Your quads are your front thigh muscles. Holding onto a chair or fence for balance, bend the right leg up behind you. Grasp the top of your foot and push it into your hand. Feel the stretch, then repeat with the left leg.

Hamstring stretch

Your hamstrings are your back thigh muscles. With your chin up, bend at the waist. Bend the right knee and hold for a few seconds, leaning on the bended leg for balance if needed. Feel the stretch in the left leg. Now straighten and bend the left knee. Repeat twice more.

Hip circles

Stand with your feet quite wide apart. Place your hands on your hips. Now slowly make big circles with your hips, first in one direction, then the other.

BEAR SAYS

You need a supple lower body and strong legs for any sport that involves rapid changes in direction, such as football, basketball, tennis, and squash.

CORE AND BALANCE

Your core is the central part of your body – your stomach, back, and bottom. Strength and flexibility in your core is vital for any exercise, as it will support the rest of your body. These exercises will improve balance, posture, and flexiblilty in your core for all-round suppleness.

Diagonal stretch

Stand with your legs wide apart. Bend down and touch your left foot with your right hand. Twist to the right as you come up, and raise your left arm high and to the right above your head. Look behind you. Repeat twice more, then stretch the opposite muscles, bending down with your left hand and raising your right.

Leg raise to front

Lie on your back with your hands by your sides, palms downwards. Slowly raise your right leg as high as it will go. Make sure you don't arch your back as you do this. Hold for three seconds, then slowly lower. Repeat twice more. Now raise your left leg in the same way, then both legs at the same time. You should feel a stretch in your lower stomach muscles.

Cat stretch

Get down on your hands and knees with your hands below the shoulders and feet below the hips. Slowly raise your head and dip your back down as far as it will go. Now slowly lower the head and arch your back as high as it will go. Repeat twice more.

Bridge

Lie on your back with your knees raised and feet flat on the floor. Holding your stomach in, lift your hips to raise the body off the ground. There should be a straight line between your hips and shoulders. Hold for three seconds, then slowly lower. Repeat.

Cobra

This pose imitates a snake called a cobra, which raises its head to strike. Lie on your stomach with elbows bent and face resting on the backs of your hands. Slowly lift the upper body off the ground and hold for two seconds. Slowly lower and repeat.

Flier

Lie on your stomach with your arms and legs stretched out in a star shape. Raise the right arm and left leg, hold for two seconds, then slowly lower. Repeat, then raise the left arm and right leg.

UPPER BODY STRENGTH

These exercises are designed to build muscle strength in your upper body, including arms, chest, and shoulders. This will be particularly useful if you want to try sports like weightlifting, rock climbing, and some martial arts.

Dips

Sit on the edge of a low bench with your legs stretched out in front. Grip the edge of the bench with knuckles facing forwards. Edge your bottom off the bench and bend your elbows to lower your bottom towards the floor. Now raise yourself back up. Repeat.

Pull-ups

Stand below a bar or low branch a little higher than your head. Grab the bar underhand, with knuckles facing outwards or inwards. Pull your body up towards the bar, then lower. Repeat. You can pick a low bar and push up a little with your legs to help you achieve the pull up if you are struggling to lift all your own weight.

BEAR SAYS

Start off doing a few of each exercise and gradually increase the number. Playing leapfrog or using a climbing frame can help to build upper body strength.

Half pull-ups

Another option if full pull-ups are too hard is to balance a broomstick or bar between two cushioned chairs. Make sure it will take your weight. Grip underhand or overhand and raise your body off the floor. Repeat.

Press-ups

Lie on your stomach with your hands below your shoulders. Straighten the arms to lift the body onto the hands and toes. The back should be straight with elbows facing backwards. Lower to just above the floor, then lift again. Repeat as many times as you can.

Half press-ups

This is similar to a press-up but the knees stay on the floor. Straighten your arms to raise the body in a straight line from knees to shoulders. Lower and lift again. Repeat.

Bicep curl

Stand up straight, holding a small weight such as a can of food or bottle of water in both hands with the weights touching your hips. Bend the elbows to raise the weights to your shoulders. Slowly lower, then repeat.

LOWER BODY STRENGTH

These exercises focus on the lower body, building muscle strength in the legs and hips. Any sport that requires running – including athletics, football, and tennis – will need a strong lower body.

Squats

Stand with your feet shoulder-width apart. Cross your hands over your chest. Bend your knees and slowly lower yourself into a squat, but don't let your bottom go lower than your knees. Hold for two seconds, then stand up again. Repeat as many times as you can.

Squat jump

Stand with the feet slightly apart and hands by your sides. Bend at the knees to touch your ankles. Now leap into the air, and land back in the squat position. Repeat as many times as you can. This also engages your calf muscles.

Forward step up

Stand facing a step or low bench. Step up with your right foot, then with your left so both feet are flat on the step. Now step down with the right and then the left. Repeat, starting with the left leg this time. Repeat the whole exercise.

Side step up

Stand at right-angles to a step with your right foot nearest the step. Step up with your right foot, then raise your body so the left foot is in the air. Step down with the left foot, then the right foot. Repeat, then face the other way and step up with the left foot first.

Star jump

Stand with your feet together and arms by your sides. Jump out into a star shape with feet and arms outstretched, then jump back again. Repeat for 30 seconds.

BEAR SAYS

Music can help you to do exercises rhythmically. It can also help to energize you during a tough workout.

Calf raise

Stand on tip-toe at the edge of a low bench, or the bottom step of a staircase. Hold onto a rail if you can. Raise yourself up on your toes, then lower as far as you can. Repeat several times.

CORE STRENGTH

The exercises on this page aim to build strength in your body core and limbs. Take care doing these strenuous exercises, as you don't want to injure yourself. These might be hard at first, but the more you do them, the better you will get.

Burpee

Stand with your feet hip-width apart and arms at your sides. Bend down to take your weight on your hands, and at the same time thrust your legs out behind you, as if doing a press-up. Jump your feet back up into a squat, stand up again, and end with a little jump. Repeat.

Sit-up

Lie on your back with your hands crossed over your chest. Anchor your feet under furniture such as a low table, or get a partner to hold your feet down. Curl your upper body up to a sitting position, then lower. Repeat. These exercises are also called curl-ups.

Plank

Lie on your stomach with elbows below your shoulders and arms facing forwards. Tighten your stomach, then lift the body off the floor so your weight is on your toes and elbows. Keep the body in a straight line. Hold for a time, then lower.

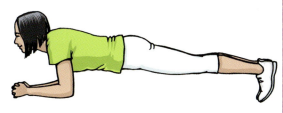

Half plank

If the plank is too hard, raise your body onto your knees and elbows. The body should form a straight line slanting from knees to shoulders. Hold for 30 seconds.

Crab

Lie on your back with your knees raised, feet flat on the floor, elbows raised and hands by your ears with palms on the floor. Now lift your trunk off the ground into the "crab" position. Can you hold this position? Can you move about carefully?

BEAR SAYS

Choose a mixture of exercises to work on strength and flexibility. Do those exercises for a week, then choose another set to work on other muscles. Always begin with warm-up stretches.

BUILDING STAMINA

The best way to increase stamina is to do aerobic exercise. This type of exercise, which gets your heart pumping and your lungs working, is also called cardiovascular exercise.

Fast walking

Experts recommend taking at least 10,000 steps a day. Buy a cheap pedometer to measure your paces, or many smartphones have a built-in app that will count your steps. You have to walk fast to make the exercise aerobic – your heartbeat should speed up slightly. Keep your head up and body upright.

BEAR SAYS

If you've never run before, start by running for two minutes and walking for three minutes, then repeat the sequence. Gradually increase the time spent running, not walking.

Running

Running is the simplest form of aerobic exercise. Start with a 5–10 minute run or cover 1–2 km. Gradually increase the time and distance. Keep your shoulders down and body upright. Running uphill strengthens the leg muscles.

Cycling

As with running, you might find it helps to start with a short bike ride and slowly increase the distance as your fitness improves. Make sure the saddle is at a comfortable height. Keep your head still and body relaxed. Include a hill to strengthen leg muscles.

Rowing

Rowing works the leg, bottom, back, and shoulder muscles, as well as being a fantastic workout for your heart and lungs. Many gyms have rowing machines, or you could look into joining a local rowing club if there is one. Keep your back straight, and ask a professional for help if you are unsure.

Swimming

Swimming tones the body with little risk of injury. Breaststroke mainly works the leg muscles. Make the strokes as long as possible. Front crawl mainly works the upper body. Breathe out underwater, then lift the head to the side to breathe.

Skipping

Skipping strengthens bones, lungs, and leg muscles. Rope skipping also tones the shoulders. You can also skip without a rope, lifting one knee high as you hop.

CIRCUIT TRAINING

Circuit training is a fast-paced workout. You do different exercises at a number of different "stations". It's a great way to get fit and strengthen muscles all over your body!

Set up your circuit

The idea is to spend 30 seconds to two minutes doing as many repetitions of an exercise at each station, then take a short, 30 second rest, then move on to the next exercise. Choose 6–10 exercises and put out any equipment you will need at different stations.

Shuttle runs

Shuttle runs are often part of circuit training. Run between two lines about 10 m apart as fast as you can, turning quickly. These short runs strengthen muscles involved in turning as well as sprinting. Again, spend 30 seconds to two minutes doing as many shuttles back and forward as you can, then take a short, 30 second rest, then move on to the next exercise.

BEAR SAYS

Move quickly between stations. Don't give yourself more than 30 seconds to recover from each exercise. You can also hop, skip, or bounce a ball between stations.

Sample workouts

Here are some suggestions for different workouts. You can also design your own circuit depending what you want to work on. Choose a mix of exercises for strength and flexibility, and always warm up first.

Aerobic workout (12 minutes)
- Warm up stretches – 2 mins
- Star jumps – 1 min
- Shuttle runs – 2 mins
- Forward step-up – 1 min
- Bicep curl – 1 min
- Squats – 1 min
- Press-ups – 1 min
- Skipping – 1 min
- Jogging on spot with high knees – 1 min
- Cool down stretches – 1 min

Flexi-workout (8 minutes)
- Neck stretch – 30 seconds
- High and low – 1 min
- Side stretch – 30 seconds
- Arm circles – 30 seconds
- Waist rotation – 30 seconds
- Diagonal stretch – 1 min
- Hip circles – 30 seconds
- Foot circles – 30 seconds
- Touch toes while sitting – 1 min
- Fast jogging on spot – 1 min
- Cat stretch – 1 min

Fun workout (12 minutes)
- Warm up stretches – 2 mins
- Hula hoop – 1 min
- Bunny hops – 1 min
- Rope skip – 2 mins
- Cartwheels or handstands – 1 min
- Ball juggling – 1 min
- Crab – 1 min
- Leapfrog or wheelbarrow race – 2 mins
- Cool down stretches – 1 min

Killer workout (12 minutes)
- Warm up stretches – 2 mins
- Burpees – 1 min
- Squat jumps – 1 min
- Shuttle runs – 2 mins
- Plank – 1 min
- Press-up – 1 min
- Side step-up – 1 min
- Pull-ups – 1 min
- Dips – 1 min
- Cool down stretches – 1 min

Bear summary

I like to do short and sharp workouts. I often use body weight exercises, performed at high intensity for short periods of time, a quick rest, then onto the next exercise. If you do this for 20–30 minutes, then spend a few minutes stretching at the end, you will build strength, aerobic fitness, and flexibility.

41

GAMES FOR FITNESS

Fun and games can help build your fitness too! Ball and flying disc games tone your muscles and improve aim and coordination, while races and other running games will build your aerobic fitness, lower body strength, and flexibility.

French cricket

You need a cricket or tennis bat and a tennis ball. One person bats, the rest are fielders. The fielders' aim is to hit the batter's legs below the knee with the ball. The batter cannot move his or her legs, but uses the bat to defend them. If the batter hits the ball, the fielder who recovers the ball bowls from that spot. If the ball is caught, the batter is out and the catcher is the next to bat.

Football or hockey

These are team sports, but you don't need loads of people to play football or hockey. Three people can take it in turns to shoot and be in goal. Four or more people can split into two teams with two goals.

Sharp shooter

Players take turns to shoot a basketball at the high hoop. If you score, you get a point. The other players have one try to score from the same position and gain a point. You then spread out and try to score from different positions. The first to 10 points wins.

Down down

You need a tennis ball. Stand in a circle and throw to one another. When a person misses a fair catch, they go down on one knee. If they manage to catch next time they stand up, but if they miss again they go down on two knees, then one elbow, two elbows and finally on the chin. If you miss on your chin you're out!

Flying disc

You need an open space. To throw the disk, stand sideways on and hold the disc flat. Pull your arm back and then flick the wrist as you throw to another player. You can catch with one or two hands or even on one finger. Throw the disk at a slight angle to curve it through the air.

Chain tag

One person is "it". When "it" tags another player, the two players link arms and chase after everyone else together. Before long, there will be a long line of catchers, all trying to catch the remaining players. The only people in the chain who can tag are the people on each end.

Stick in the mud

Choose one or two people to be "it". When the catcher tags you, you have to stand still with your legs apart. You can be freed if another person crawls through your legs. Choose another catcher when everyone is stuck.

Fun races

Races such wheelbarrow, egg and spoon, sack, and three-legged races are all great for building endurance – and a lot of fun! Why not come up with lots of different races and split your friends or classmates into two or more teams for a sports day?

Ball relay

You need two teams, a selection of balls of different sizes, two hula hoops, and two sacks. Place each team's balls inside the hula hoop and the sack at the far end. Each player picks up one ball, races to the far end, and puts it in the sack, then races back again. The last player picks up the sack and brings it back. When all the balls are safely back in the hoop, that team has won.

Sponge relay

You need two sponges and four buckets. Each team has a sponge and full bucket of water, with an empty bucket at the far end. Each player has to take a sponge full of water to the far end, wring it into the empty bucket and race back. Speed is important, but the team with the most water in the far bucket wins.

Leapfrog

Leapfrog can be a fun relay game. Everyone but the last player bends over with their hands on their knees. The last player hops over everyone in front, then takes their position at the front of the line. The new person at the back of the line goes next. You win when all your team have hopped.

GLOSSARY

Aerobic – Exercise that requires oxygen, which makes the heart and lungs work harder.

Alveoli (singular: alveolus) – The tiny air sacs in the lungs which allow oxygen to seep from the air into the blood, and carbon dioxide to seep out.

Anaerobic – Exercise that requires more oxygen that is supplied by breathing, which makes the body release stored oxygen.

Artery – One of the large blood vessels that carry blood from the heart to the rest of the body.

Asthma – An illness which causes difficulties with breathing.

Biceps – The muscles in the upper arm that flex the elbow.

Capillary – A tiny blood vessel.

Carbohydrates – A group of nutrients found in foods such as fruit, vegetables, and grains. Carbohydrates provide much of our energy.

Cardiovascular – Relating to the heart and blood vessels.

Contract – To get shorter.

Diabetes – An illness which results in abnormal sugar levels in the blood.

Endorphin – One of a group of natural body chemicals that produce feelings of well-being.

Hamstrings – The tendons at the back of the knee.

Immune system – The organs and chemicals in the body that fight infection and disease.

Inhaler – A medical device that delivers medicine which helps people with asthma breathe more easily.

Metabolism – The natural processes that take place within the body to maintain life.

Nutrient – A substance that provides nourishment.

Pedometer – An instrument that measures the number of steps you take.

Protein – A nutrient found in foods such as meat, fish, milk, eggs, nuts, and beans, that allows cells and the body to work.

Quadriceps – The large muscle in the front of the thigh that helps to flex the leg.

Resting pulse – The pulse or heart rate when a person is resting.

Stamina – The ability to keep going during physical exercise.

Tendon – A stretchy fibre that connects a muscle to a bone.

Triceps – The muscles in the upper arm that straighten the elbow.

Vein – One of the large blood vessels that carry blood from the body back to the heart and lungs.

Discover more amazing books in the Bear Grylls series:

Perfect for young adventurers, the *Survival Skills* series accompanies an exciting range of colouring and activity books. Curious kids can also learn tips and tricks for almost any extreme situation in *Survival Camp*, explore Earth in *Extreme Planet*, and discover some of history's greatest explorers in the *Epic Adventures* series.

Conceived by Weldon Owen in partnership with Bear Grylls Ventures

Produced by Weldon Owen, an imprint of Kings Road Publishing
Suite 3.08 The Plaza, 535 Kings Road,
London SW10 0SZ, UK

WELDON OWEN
Editor Susie Rae
Designer Shahid Mahmood
Contributor Jen Green
Illustrator Julian Baker
Cover image © Ben Simms 2018
Printed in Malaysia
2 4 6 8 10 9 7 5 3 1

Disclaimer
Weldon Owen and Bear Grylls take pride in doing our best to get the facts right in putting together the information in this book, but occasionally something slips past our beady eyes. Therefore we make no warranties about the accuracy or completeness of the information in the book and to the maximum extent permitted, we disclaim all liability. Wherever possible, we will endeavour to correct any errors of fact at reprint.

Kids – if you want to try any of the activities in this book, please ask your parents first! Parents – all outdoor activities carry some degree of risk and we recommend that anyone participating in these activities be aware of the risks involved and seek professional instruction and guidance. None of the health/medical information in this book is intended as a substitute for professional medical advice; always seek the advice of a qualified practitioner.

A WELDON OWEN PRODUCTION. AN IMPRINT OF KINGS ROAD PUBLISHING.
PART OF THE BONNIER PUBLISHING GROUP.

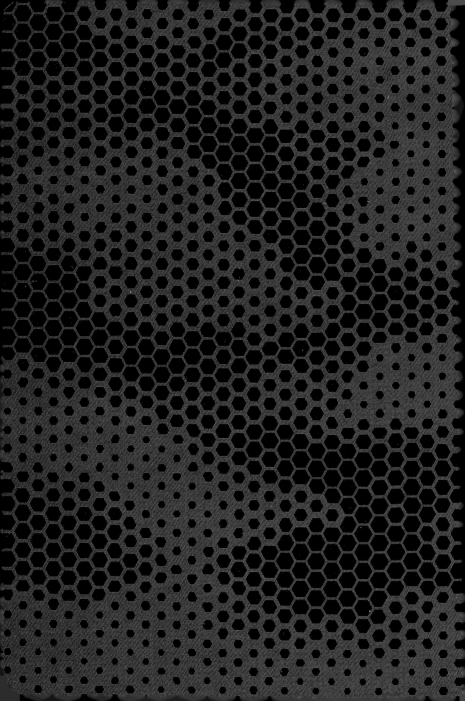